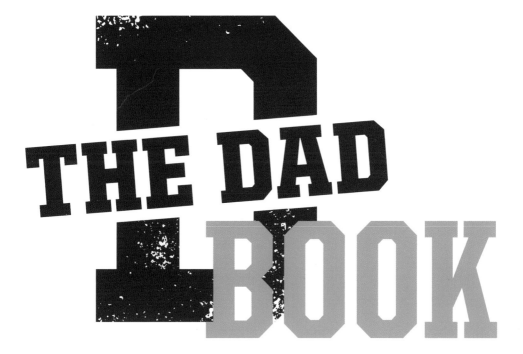

THE DAD BOOK

Being a father
is the most rewarding
job in the world.
Unless of course you
have a job where the
reward is cash.

THE DAD BOOK

TRUTHS, HACKS, AND DAD-ISMS

Edited by Joel Willis and Ally Probst

My kids might not be the smartest, they might not be the best looking, but I sure as hell have forgotten where I was going with this...

The Dad Book. Copyright © 2019 by Some Spider, Inc. All rights reserved. Published by The Dad, a division of Some Spider, Inc. This book or any portion thereof may not be reproduced or used in any manner whatsoever without the express written permission of the publisher. First Printing, 2019. Design by Mike Essl. ISBN: 978-1-7330894-0-1. Printed in the United States of America.

Parenting:
some days you bask in
the adulation of
unconditional love and
some days you clean sh*t
out of the bathtub.

WELCOME TO THE CLUB

When I find out that a friend is going to be a dad, I slap him on the back and say, "Welcome to the club, man." Parenthood is a club and membership is lifelong. Nothing will ever be the same again.

We started The Dad as a place for modern dads to laugh with a community of people who get it. We are the guys who have been puked on and yelled at by tyrannical tiny humans. We are the diaper changers, the spider killers, the bedtime story tellers. We are threatening to turn this car around if the kids don't knock it off. And when we see a parent struggling with a toddler throwing a tantrum, we don't judge, because we've been there. We will probably be there again, later today. We're all in this together.

If you're looking for actual, helpful parenting advice, you won't find it in this book. What you will find is entertainment, absurdity, and solidarity. This is the dad life.

Welcome to parenthood.

You're about to spend an irrational amount of time convincing a sleepy person to go to sleep.

NEW DADS

There's nothing like the feeling of holding your newborn for the first time. The love, the awe, the terrifying realization that this small screaming stranger is your problem now. What a cute bundle of joy and needs. The nurse hands this kid over to you, as if you have any idea what you're doing. Ready or not, here comes fatherhood.

And worst of all, when they kick you out of the hospital, they don't even include an owner's manual. Sure, LEGO sets come with step-by-step instructions, but not this entire human being. It'll be fine... probably? The good news is that none of us know what we are doing at the beginning, we are all equally overwhelmed. Nothing could have prepared us for this tiny new roommate that yells all night, throws up habitually, and doesn't even pay rent.

In new parent mode, the goal is to adapt and survive. Because while the initiation into the dad club comes with a whole new kind of love, it also comes with a whole new level of tired.

MATERNITY WARD

DOCTOR: So baby's on the way? How's your wife?

ME: She is fine but we are a bit nervous.

DOCTOR: Contractions?

ME: Sorry. She's fine but we're a bit nervous.

Now that I'm a dad
I'm thinking of going back to
my old shop class.

"Oh, hey Mr. Peterson,
remember when you made fun
of me for not being able to make
a spice rack? Look who made
AN ENTIRE PERSON!"

THE LIFE OF A PARENT

■ Feeling overwhelmed with love
■ Feeling overwhelmed with stress
■ Wingin' it

WIFE: Wow, you swaddled him perfectly on your first try. You're a natural father.

ME: [after years of perfecting my burrito wrapping technique] Sure, let's go with that.

When you become a father, it's like someone instantly fills your heart with love and your car with crumbs.

Baby >

Goodnight!

Goodnight buddy, see you in the morning

Lol!

What?

FYI I plan to wake up like 6 times tonight. K?

Wait, no. 😱 Why?

Idk 🙌

See you soon 🐣

Ugh

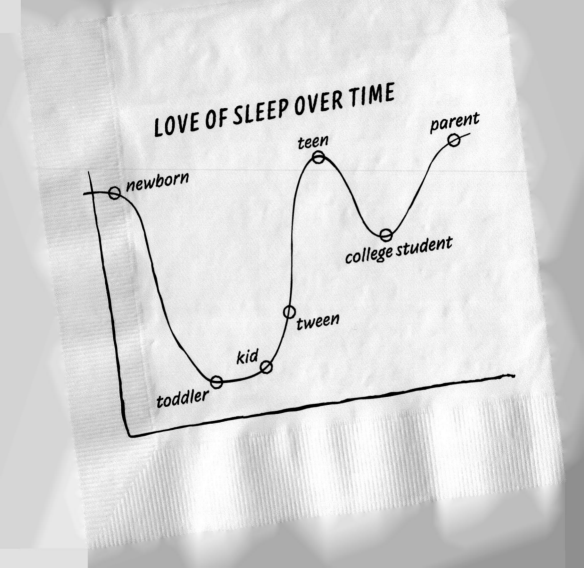

LOVE OF SLEEP OVER TIME

newborn

toddler

kid

tween

teen

college student

parent

ONE OF THE HARDEST THINGS ABOUT BEING A PARENT IS THE PART WHEN THEY'RE AWAKE.

If you see me looking tired, you don't need to point it out. Nobody knows better than me just how little sleep I got last night.

BABIES

DADS

WANTING TO
STAY HOME AND NAP

Hey guys, thanks for inviting me out for drinks tonight but do you remember a couple of months ago I had that baby?

Well, he's still around, so no.

LOVE LANGUAGES FOR NEW PARENTS

ACTS OF SERVICE
"Let me watch the kids so you can nap."

QUALITY TIME
Spending more time napping.

WORDS OF AFFIRMATION
"You deserve a nap."

PHYSICAL TOUCH
Your face hitting the pillow for a nap.

RECEIVING GIFTS
"Here's a blanket now go take a nap."

NEWTON'S LAW OF PARENTING

An adult at rest can never stay at rest without being acted upon by kid forces.

I'M SO TIRED.

HOW TIRED ARE YOU?

I'M SO TIRED

the bags under my eyes
are filled with other bags like
the plastic grocery bags
my wife keeps under the sink.

Wife: I underestimated how much crying there would be when we had a kid.

Me: *dabbing my eyes* It's just really hard some days, ok?

IMPOSSIBLY DIFFICULT

100% WORTH IT

Folding a
fitted sheet

The water level
from the Ninja
Turtles game
on Nintendo

PARENTING

Using the right
tool for the job

Naps

Spelling
restaurant
right on the
first try

Spending more
for good beer

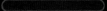

Baby >

Hey dad...

Oh no, what is it?

Just wanted to let you know
I'm about to blow out my diaper
 in a big way

What? No! You just did that an
hour ago! It's not possible!

It's happening. Right. Now.

Baby >

I don't understand. You don't even eat solid food! 😣 Ugh fine. I'll get the wipes.

Better bring two packs

And run a bath 😎

This better be the last time you sh*t yourself today

No promises my dude

Baby: *crying for 3 hours*

Me: Okay good chat.

WHEN MY KID IS BORN

I can't wait for him to walk and talk.

WHEN MY KID STARTS TO WALK AND TALK

Okay stop now.

INVENTION OF BABIES

GOD: Ok so, make them neediest during their first year, but don't give them any comprehensible language skills until, like, way later lol

ANGEL: *Noticeably distressed*

Being a dad feels like being a superhero whose superpower is somehow loving someone despite them being a total dick 90% of the time.

First birthday parties should be celebrations of the parents. You create a human, keep it alive for an entire year, then people act like it's some big accomplishment for the kid?

No thanks.

I'M SO TIRED.

HOW TIRED ARE YOU?

I'M SO TIRED

I thought I had mono
but it turns out
I just have a baby.

MY FAVORITE PART OF PARENTING IS ALWAYS HAVING SOMEONE AROUND WHO DOESN'T YET REALIZE THAT I AM A DEEPLY FLAWED INDIVIDUAL.

When you saw only one set of footprints in the sand, it was then that I had to carry my scream-crying kid inside from the beach for a nap.

That moment when you're forced to watch your kid's favorite TV show then you realize he wandered off half an hour ago and you're sitting there enjoying it on your own.

INSIDE A
TODDLER'S BRAIN

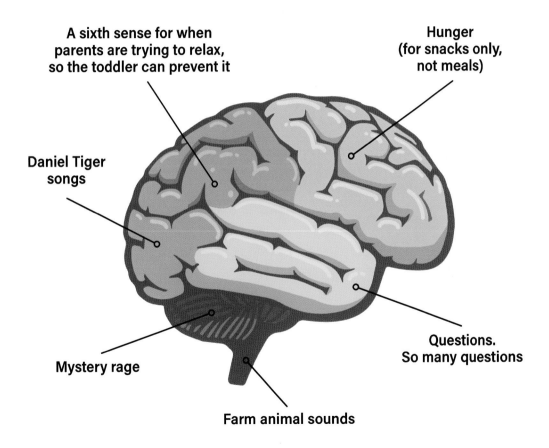

A sixth sense for when
parents are trying to relax,
so the toddler can prevent it

Hunger
(for snacks only,
not meals)

Daniel Tiger
songs

Mystery rage

Farm animal sounds

Questions.
So many questions

I AM SO ANGRY RIGHT NOW
😡😡😡

Why? What's the matter pal?

I'LL NEVER TELL!!!!! I AM JUST
GONNA SCREEEEAM UNTIL
EVERYONE STARES AT US

Aww, how about I try to give
you a hug and tell you it's
okay? 🥰

Toddler >

I WILL TRY TO KICK YOU WITH
MY TINY NINJA FOOT 🤬

> Okay cool it. Take it easy. Here,
> I'll give you your favorite toy?

Omg 🤮 that toy? I HATE THAT
TOY NOW (I just decided)

> Want a donut? I'll get you
> one with spriiiinkles

🙂 🙂 😊 😄 🤗 🤗 🤗

39

I'M SO TIRED.

HOW TIRED ARE YOU?

I'M SO TIRED

I'm eating coffee grounds
out of a bowl like cereal.

2-DAY-OLD BABY

HE'S SO QUIET, GO AND CHECK IF HE'S ALIVE.

2-YEAR-OLD KID

HE'S SO QUIET, IF YOU WAKE HIM I'LL KILL YOU.

Don't sugarcoat life for your baby.

When you do that "here comes the airplane" thing with their food, be sure to include a 3-hour layover in Dallas.

DADVICE

Right from the beginning, it's clear that this parenthood thing isn't going to be easy. It's basically an impossible task, but we do it anyway. Fortunately, dads are nothing if not resourceful. Armed with duct tape and super glue, we figure it out. We learn to fix boo-boos, cars, houses, and broken hearts. We do whatever needs to be done. Along the way, we find shortcuts. We learn the secrets of the dad trade, and then pass these life lessons on to others. Nothing is more valuable than wise advice from a knowledgeable father.

Unfortunately, we don't have wise advice to offer you here. If you're looking for useful information, call your dad or pick up literally any other parenting book. What we do have are truths about kid behavior that we offer no solution to, unhelpful instructions we made up, and ill-advised dad hacks you probably shouldn't try at home. Gather 'round, dads, for some dadvice that comes with absolutely no guarantees.

Dadle

KID TRANSLATION

| Kids | Spanish | French | English |

Dad, can I sit on your lap?

| English | Spanish | Arabic | **Translate** |

Dad, I'm about to crush your nuts with my knee.

WE OWE IT TO OUR CHILDREN TO LOOK THEM IN THE EYE, TELL THEM HOW MUCH THEY MEAN TO US, AND LET THEM KNOW WHEN THEY REALLY SUCK AT SOMETHING.

DAD HACK

Fill the piñata with goat intestines to teach children about the brutal consequences of violence.

DAD HACK

Tell your kid the new season of Caillou just came out and turn on Poltergeist. Now you never have to watch Caillou again.

6 EXERCISES FOR DADS

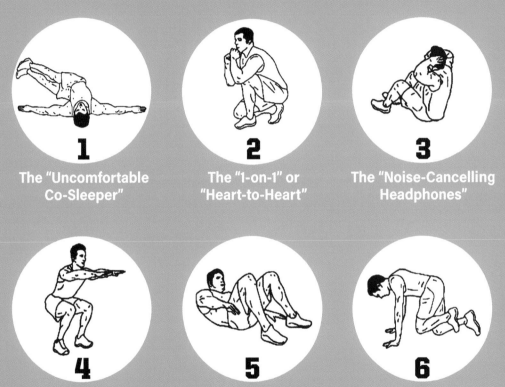

1 The "Uncomfortable Co-Sleeper"

2 The "1-on-1" or "Heart-to-Heart"

3 The "Noise-Cancelling Headphones"

4 The "Look How Tall You Are"

5 The "Cargo Shorts Check"

6 The "Got Me Right In The 'Nads"

HOW TO

SALVAGE YOUR WALL WHEN YOUR KID DRAWS ON IT

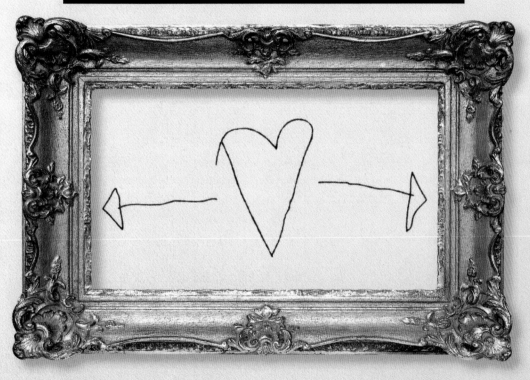

Jack (b. 2010)
Valentine's Decoration
Crayon on wall
He drew this to celebrate Valentine's Day
and his parents are going with it.

DAD HACK

I play "Cinderella" with my daughter. She's Cinderella and I'm Drizella and I yell at her until she cleans the whole house.

"Cool, Buddy."

When you stopped listening to your kid's rambling 10 minutes ago but now they've paused for a response.

Dadle

KID TRANSLATION

| Kids | Spanish | French | English |

> Dad, can you read me a book before bed tonight?

| English | Spanish | Arabic | Translate |

> Dad, can you read me 6 books, do 2 crossword puzzles, sing 4 songs, and complete a book of Mad Libs with me before bed tonight?

HOW TO

ENCOURAGE INDEPENDENCE

Move your child's bed 1 inch farther from your room every night and before they notice they are living next door and no longer your responsibility.

DAD HACK

AMERICA Online

Dialing...

Build character by making your kids stare at this for five minutes before they can use the wifi.

HOW TO

GET YOUR KIDS TO PICK UP THEIR GARBAGE

FOUND

String cheese wrapper on the floor

Pick it up: in the same damn spot you left it

Reward: throw it in the trash and if I don't find another one for a week, I'll give you the new wifi password

Hang this on your fridge.

I hope you have an AMAZING ~~Thursday.~~ FRIDAY
I love you so much! ☺
Love,
~~Mommy~~
DADDY

Reuse school lunchbox notes.

Dadle

KID TRANSLATION

| Kids | Spanish | French | English |

Dad, can I try your ice cream?

| English | Spanish | Arabic | **Translate** |

Dad, your ice cream is mine now.

HOW TO

TEACH YOUR KID SOMETHING NEW

**Using candy as a reward can be helpful.
You can even offer the kid some if you want.**

DAD HACK

If you occasionally yell "I wonder where they are" while your kids are hiding during hide and seek, you can get a remarkable amount of things done around the house in peace.

Wife, lecturing son:
You can't just "wing it"
your entire life.

Me, later to my
son when we're alone:
You actually can just
wing it, you just can't tell
people that's what
you're doing.

HOW TO

GET KIDS TO CLEAN UP

Make it fun! Play "the floor is lava." If the kids leave their toys on the floor, set them on fire.

DAD HACK

Show your kid how much they absolutely nailed that drawing they made of you by photoshopping it into an actual family picture.

Parents are allowed to be hypocrites. For example, I tell my kids it's wrong to lie AND that their favorite annoying online video was destroyed in a fire at the internet factory.

DAD HACK

Get your kids interested in LEGOs because it's the only socially acceptable way you can still play with LEGOs.

**Figured out how to get my kids
to stop messing with the thermostat.**

Son: Why do people have kids?

Me: Well buddy, when a man and a woman loathe free time and discretionary income very very much...

EXPERT DADS

After you have learned the fatherhood controls and the rules of the game, you level up to "expert dad." While there are plenty of new achievements to unlock along the way, you aren't a newbie anymore. Things no one ever told you about parenthood are now second nature. Although parenting never gets easier, we become more skilled with time. Or maybe more numb. We don't know, we're too tired to tell.

Life with kids is crazy, but eventually it becomes a familiar, comfortable kind of crazy. Expert dads know how to make some sense out of the pure chaos of parenting. It's a rodeo, but it ain't your first one.

Parenting is equal parts "oh my god they're just like me" in happiness and "oh my god they're just like me" in terror.

POINT ON THE CHART

SON: I'm tired, Dad.

ME: Me too, buddy.

WIFE: *gasps*

ME: I MEAN "HI TIRED, I'M DAD."

WIFE, ALREADY ON WITH 911, CRYING:
No this has never happened before, please hurry.

ACHIEVEMENT UNLOCKED

Completed a home improvement project with only 1 trip to the hardware store.

Nobody ever tells you how much of parenting is spent pretending to be impressed by bad art.

FIRST KID

Oh no did you get an owie?
Poor thing, let's get you a band-aid.

SECOND KID

Don't bother me unless there's an
elevators-opening-in-The-Shining
amount of blood.

Me: There's nothing I wouldn't do for my child. I would walk through the fires of hell and back for him.

Son: Can we go to the park?

Me: No, it's raining a little bit.

ACHIEVEMENT UNLOCKED

Packed 95% of the house into the trunk for a weekend trip.

DAD

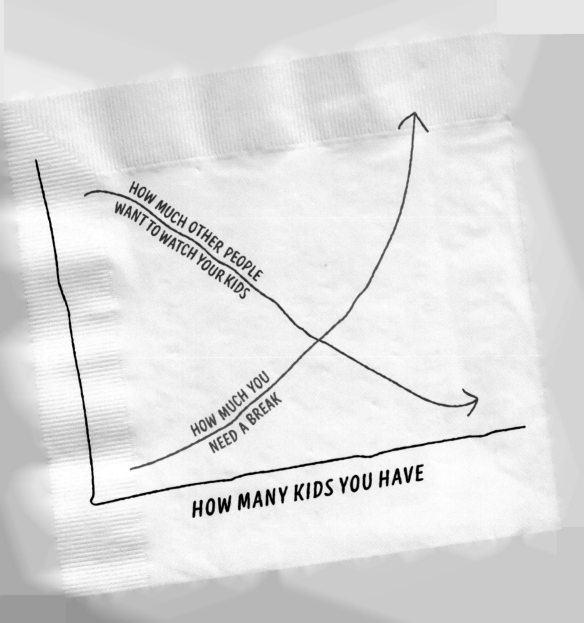

**Came home and thought someone broke in
and trashed the place to send a message
then I remembered I have kids.**

FIRST KID

Of course I'll stay with you at the birthday party. I don't know the parents very well yet and I'd like to get to know them.

SECOND KID

I'm not even gonna park at Chuck E Cheese so get ready to jump out as we roll past. I'll pick you up in a few hours, probably.

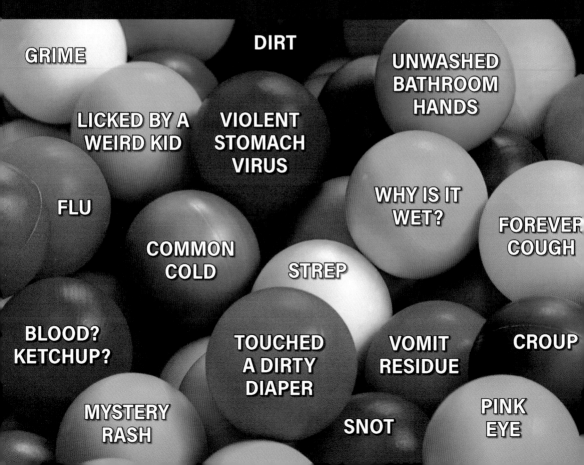

★ EXPERT DADS KNOW ★

What's really in the ball pit.

GRIME

DIRT

UNWASHED BATHROOM HANDS

LICKED BY A WEIRD KID

VIOLENT STOMACH VIRUS

FLU

WHY IS IT WET?

FOREVER COUGH

COMMON COLD

STREP

BLOOD? KETCHUP?

TOUCHED A DIRTY DIAPER

VOMIT RESIDUE

CROUP

MYSTERY RASH

SNOT

PINK EYE

ME TELLING A STORY vs **MY KID TELLING A STORY**

**When you're playing hide and seek
with your kid and realize you won't need
that college fund after all.**

WHY WE REALLY MAKE OUR KIDS WEAR COATS

- To keep them warm on the 15 second walk from the car into school
- So they don't "catch a cold"
- So I don't get judged

WHAT WE SAY

Please share with your brother.

WHAT THEY HEAR

Fight! Fight it out!
If he tries to take one
of your things, make him
cry with your fists!

ACHIEVEMENT UNLOCKED

Carried in more than $200
of groceries in a single trip.

My kids are so open to experiencing culture.
They'll try anything, from chicken tenders
at a Mexican restaurant to chicken tenders
at a Mediterranean restaurant.

BEFORE I HAD KIDS I DIDN'T EVEN KNOW YOU COULD CUT A SANDWICH "WRONG."

EATING AT A RESTAURANT WITH KIDS

■ Yelling at kids to sit back down
■ Waiting for the check
■ Eating

Your child would like a snack even though they just refused all their food at dinner 7 minutes ago

 Don't ask me again

Don't Allow   OK

I wish I could hit
"don't ask me again"
in real life.

Sometimes being a dad is serving yourself the worst pancakes, because the real pleasure is seeing your kids enjoy the good ones.

SON: Wait daddy,
this isn't our normal ketchup.
screaming
I WANT MY KETCHUUUUUUP!

ME: *sipping my expensive
craft beer exclusively brewed
by monks in a remote village*
Oh don't make a fuss,
they're all the same.

WHAT WE SAY

It's time to sleep now.

WHAT THEY HEAR

It's time to ask for a drink of water, decide your pajamas are itchy, and ask me philosophical questions about your mortality.

COULD BE GHOSTS, COULD BE KIDS

- Shadowy form standing over my bed
- Creepy giggling coming from upstairs
- Unintelligible whispers
- Ever-present anxiety and paranoia
- Objects vanishing mysteriously
- Putrid smell from an unknown source

with toy tools and toy appliances? Like, buddy, this is the one time in your life you don't have to do sh*t, why you wanna pretend to repair the washing machine and cook fake pancakes?

THE ELEVATOR BUTTONS PARENTS NEED

THE MOVIE RATING SYSTEM PARENTS NEED

G+	**Made for kids but adults will like it too.**
G-	**Kids will love it but has an annoying soundtrack you'll have to listen to for a year straight.**
PG+	**There's a good dog in this.**
PG-	**The dog dies at the end.**
PG-13+	**Some violence but it's just people killing robots/aliens so it doesn't count.**
PG-13-	**Oh no this is way too sexual to watch with your family, everyone will feel super awkward.**

GOD: Welcome to Heaven!

ME: Heaven is a bathroom?

GOD: Try it.

ME: There...there's no kids banging on the door.

GOD: *Smiles* No, there's not.

ME: *Tearing up* Thank you.

WEEKEND OUTLOOK FOR PARENTS

FRIDAY	SATURDAY	SUNDAY
HECK YES, IT'S FAMILY TIME.	THESE KIDS ARE GETTIN' ON MY DANG NERVES.	MAYBE KIDS SHOULD GO TO SCHOOL ON WEEKENDS TOO?
LOW 62°	LOW 58°	

WHEN I'M TRYING TO WALK AROUND IN MY HOUSE

Tripping over shoes nonstop because kids leave them everywhere.

WHEN I'M TRYING TO GET KIDS OUT OF THE HOUSE

No shoes to be found, a barren shoeless desert, a tumbleweed rolls by.

THE DAD: Hey kids, gather 'round. I'd like to share a classic film from my childhood that literally changed my life and shaped who I am as a person.

THE KID: This is boring.

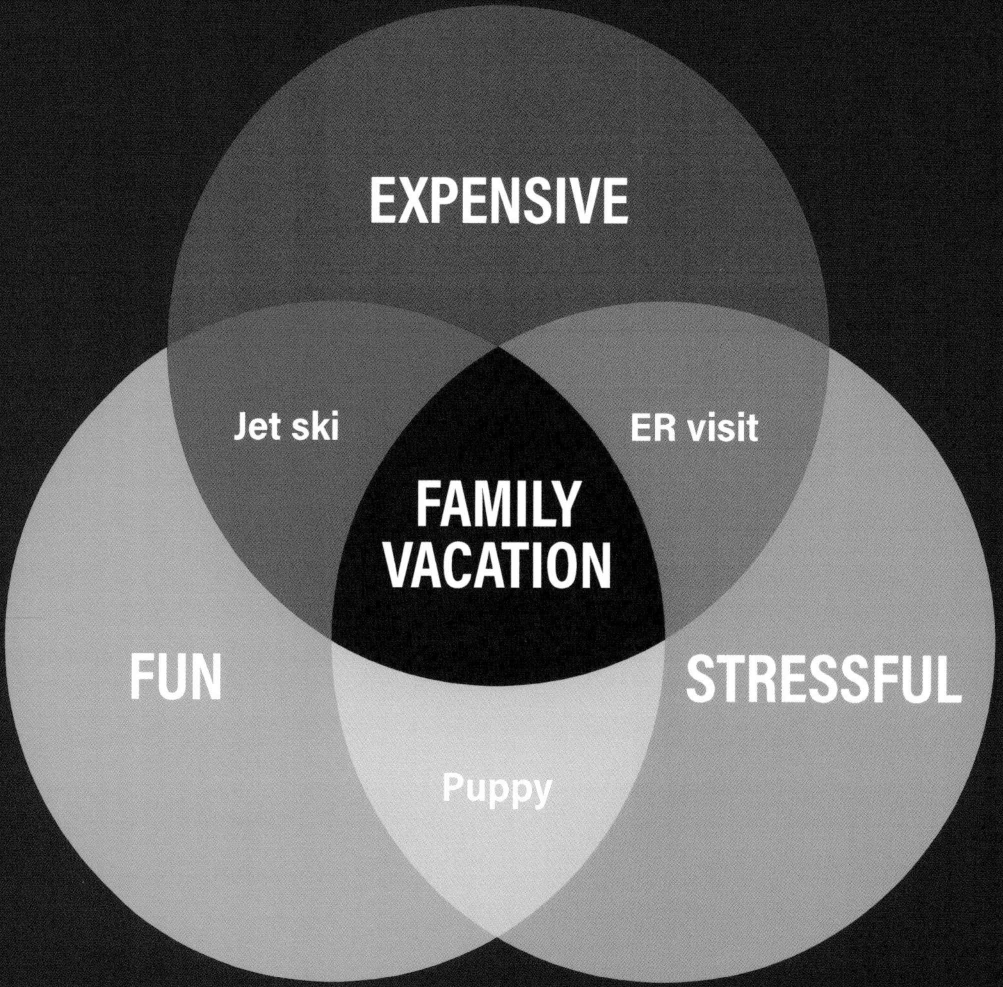

EXPENSIVE

FUN

STRESSFUL

Jet ski

ER visit

FAMILY VACATION

Puppy

ACHIEVEMENT UNLOCKED
Got kids to bed
without mumbling more
than 3 cuss words.

90% of the reason I wanted kids is because if you don't know something you can just make up whatever you want and they'll stare at you like you're a genius.

FIRST KID

My children will only eat home-cooked meals with organic ingredients.

SECOND KID

into McDonald's drive-thru speaker
"Yeah, we'll have the usual."

WHAT WE SAY

Smile for the picture please,
I just want ONE good one.

WHAT THEY HEAR

Try to make your face
as abnormal as possible,
like a pained alien.

It's not vacation
until dad loses his wallet
and calls everyone
a motherf*cker
under his breath.

FAMILY ROAD TRIP

⟳ Rage wait in the car for 15 minutes while your family tries to get out of the freakin door

➤ Take I-275W to KY-9

ⓘ Your wife forgot her charger. Debate losing 30 minutes to go back for it vs buying a new one

↑ Continue on KY-9

⚠ Your son needs to pee even though he just went 15 minutes ago

➤ Get on I-64E in Grayson from KY-9 S

⚠ Your daughter's iPad is dead and she's whining about it. Scream "CAN'T YOU ENTERTAIN YOURSELF FOR A LITTLE BIT!" at the top of your lungs

🚶 Continue on I-64E to Virginia Beach

ⓘ Answer the question "How many more minuuuuuuutes?" so many times you aren't sure time is real anymore

↰ Arrive at your destination

🍺 Have a drink or two

Nobody ever tells you how much of parenting is just standing in a parking lot waiting for your kid to get out of the car.

Kids could be having the best time ever and still ask:
What are we doing after this?

CHILDLESS FRIEND
Dude our cat
is so destructive.
It's gonna ruin
our couch someday.

ME, PULLING A BOX OF MELTED CRAYONS AND A SHATTERED IPAD OUT OF THE DRYER
Oh wow sorry
to hear that man.

Nobody ever tells you how much of parenting is swearing under your breath and counting down to bedtime.

Kid: Nice grasp on sanity you've got there, Dad.

**Would be a shame if something were to
dumps a huge bucket of toys on the ground
...happen to it.**

Wife: We should child-proof the house.

Me: Sure. Wait until they go to school and then you lock the doors and I'll nail the windows shut.

KIDS

I have to go potty but I'm
going to say I don't have to go.

DADS

I don't have to go potty
but I'm going to go sit on the toilet
for 20 minutes because it's
the only alone time I get.

GUY WITHOUT KIDS

Did you just say "potty"?

Listening to hardcore gangsta rap after dropping my kids off at school, in order to detox from the Lego Movie 2 soundtrack.

I want to put every dude with a "#1 Dad" mug into a stadium and let them fight to the death.

DAD-ISMS

"I won't be a lame dad," you promised yourself. "I'll be cool, I'll never be like my old man." Then one day you tweak your back putting on your yard work sneakers and it hits you like the heating bill in January: you've gone FULL DAD.

There is nothing to fear, it happens to all of us. We use phrases we vowed we'd never use and tell jokes we swore we'd never tell. Instinct triggers our drive to protect the important things: our offspring, lawns, and thermostats. We jump at any chance to use a pun, and what's worse is we genuinely think we're funny. It's enough to drive a man mad, but we aren't mad, just disappointed.

These are the classic dad-isms that we can't hold back anymore. We are power-less against them. But once we give in to the dad side, we discover absolute freedom. We now have access to the entire catalog of dad-isms. Cliches, bad dance moves, purposeful embarrassment, bringing up the good ole days: it's all fair game now. It's all part of being the dad.

You either die young or live long enough to see yourself bec... your own... ... flashing lights, yelling at kids to pick up their toys, muttering cuss words under your breath.

WALKED INTO A DAD CONVENTION AND SAID MICROWAVED FOOD TASTES BETTER THAN GRILLED FOOD AND A GUY THREW A CHAIR AT ME. 3 DADS VOMITED.

When you're in the car with a dad and drive past a shopping center: "I remember when this all used to be cornfields."

♥ DADS LOVE SAYING... ♥

"CAN YOU DO MINE NEXT?"
when they see a neighbor
washing his car.

"GUESS IT'S FREE THEN"
if a cashier has trouble
scanning an item.

"THEY DON'T MAKE 'EM LIKE THEY USED TO"
after anything breaks
for any reason whatsoever.

IMPORTANT:
Read Before Using

IMPORTANT :
Lire avant usage

IMPORTANTE:
Leer antes de usar

Operating/Safety Instructions
Consignes de fonctionnement/sécurité
Instrucciones de funcionamiento y seguridad

DAD LAW

Before operating, you MUST give it at least two squeezes to rev it up. Otherwise, the dad gods will curse your family and bring shame to your name.

For English
See page 2

Parlez-vous français?
Voir page 16

¿Habla español?
Ver página 30

DADS HAVE TO PEE ON ROAD TRIPS SOMETIMES TOO. WE JUST KNOW THAT IF WE CAN OUTLAST ONE OF YOU WE CAN BLAME YOU FOR STOPPING.

WHEN DADS SAY
I'LL THINK ABOUT IT

THEY REALLY MEAN
NO WAY IN HELL

**Dads love standing on the deck
staring into the distance with their
hands on their hips after a good mow.**

DAD LAW

When a little kid shakes your hand you have to pretend it was super strong:

"Whoa there, pal. Almost broke my hand haha."

"Take it easy, big guy. :)"

DADS

Laughing at fart jokes

Falling asleep on the couch

HOPING FOR HOT DOGS FOR DINNER

KIDS

DOGS

Eating things off the floor

When a dad runs into one of his coworkers out in public:

"Who let this guy in here?"

"Shouldn't you be working?"

"Guess they'll let anyone in this place."

"Haha I'm just pulling your leg. How's the family?"

TOP 5 DAD NOISES

5. Grunt getting up from the couch

4. Unintelligible answers to 6am weekend questions

3. "Ahhhh!" after sipping any beverage

2. Mumbled cuss words under breath while looking for something

1. Inexplicably loud sneezes

DAD LAW

When using a
stud finder, you must hold
it against yourself and say
"found one."

"YOU MAKE A BETTER DOOR THAN YOU DO A WINDOW"
when someone is standing in front of the TV.

"WELL THAT WAS FAST"
when someone leaves to go somewhere but comes right back because they forgot something.

"CHICKEN BUTT"
when a kid says "Guess what?"

Every dad driving by traffic going the other way:

"Good thing we're not over there!"

WHEN DADS SAY

IT BUILDS CHARACTER

THEY REALLY MEAN

IT'S GONNA SUCK

SON: Dad, why can't I have some of your special drink?

DAD: Because you still have your hopes and dreams, and you don't have a boss that pushes you to the edge every single day. Also, it's too spicy.

"YOU GOT THIS ONE?"
to a kid when
the check comes.

"WHAT'S THE DAMAGE?"
before looking at a bill.

"THAT'S HOW THEY GET YOU"
after declining additional
warranty protection.

Every pair of Dad Jeans comes with patented "What's Wrong Kiddo" technology allowing you the flexibility to pop a squat and get on your lil dude or dudette's level for an impromptu gab sesh.

GOLD STARS
FOR DADS

Mowed the lawn at 7am, waking the neighbors

Tricked a kid into saying "What's updog?"

Kids listened the first time

Played nicely with other dads

Fixed it without needing to call a guy

♥ DADS LOVE SAYING... ♥

"DID YOU FALL IN?"
when someone takes a long
time in the bathroom.

"CAN'T GET VERY FAR WITHOUT THESE"
when they come right back
in the house after
forgetting their car keys.

"LET'S ROCK AND ROLL"
when it's time to leave.

THE DAD

DAD LAW

If the princess ballerina is injured in a tragic unicorn accident and the only way to save the kingdom is to find an alternate who knows the moves then YOU STEP UP AND SAVE THE FREAKIN' KINGDOM.

Waiter: Do you wanna box for that sir?

Me: No, but I'll wrestle you for it!

I just opened up my
cargo pants pocket to reveal
an even smaller pocket
and all the neighborhood dads
just lined up to pledge
fealty by offering me
their grill tongs.

WHEN DADS SAY
IT'S A LITTLE ON THE WELL DONE SIDE.

THEY REALLY MEAN
I RUINED IT. IT'S CHARCOAL, COMPLETELY INEDIBLE.

Are you even a dad at a family meal if you don't pull this hilarious prank?

Tells joke to wife

Silence

Repeats joke to wife

Wife: Oh no, I heard you.

MARRIED WITH CHILDREN

Families come in all shapes and sizes, just like dads. Single or married, divorced or widowed, we are all part of the club.

Without a doubt, single parents are heroes who walk among us. If you know one, buy them a drink, or three. But if you have a partner joining you on your parenting journey then you know having kids changes your relationship big-time, for better and for worse.

Your spouse is your most trusted ally in the battle against the kids, but also the most likely to call you out on your crap. Your biggest fan and your loudest heckler. How can you be crazy in love with someone who just plain drives you crazy? No one knows how it works when it works. It's one of life's great mysteries. Along the way you may pick up a few marriage tricks, but expert husbands know: there's actually no such thing as an expert husband. You'll be learning on the job, forever. Figuring out parenting together can be a chaotic mess, but we're used to those.

WIFE: You don't have to do this.
I'm sure there's another way.

ME: We both know this is our only option... I love you.

WIFE: *eyes welling up with tears* I love you too.

ME: *crawls into the McDonalds PlayPlace
tube to get my crying kid out*

Wife: Did you remember to...

Me: Nope.

Wife: We need baby formula.

Me: Uh, I THINK we know how to make a baby already.

ROSES ARE RED

VIOLETS ARE BLUE

TONIGHT WHEN THE KIDS ARE IN BED

WE CAN WATCH SOMETHING THAT ISN'T CARS 2

Wife: "Let's get crazy tonight."

Husband: "Oh hell yeah. Instead of falling asleep watching The Office, let's fall asleep watching a new show."

BEFORE KIDS

A NIGHTLY SUPPORTIVE CONVERSATION ABOUT EACH OTHER'S DAYS.

AFTER KIDS

A RUTHLESS NIGHTLY COMPETITION TO PROVE WHO IS MORE TIRED FROM THEIR DAY.

MARRIAGE SEX SCHEDULE

YEAR 1

Wooooo, 4th time this week!

YEAR 10

Oh boy it's Thursday,
gettin' lucky tonight!

YEAR 25

It's the 3rd Tuesday in March,
there is a waning crescent moon,
tonight we lay.

Me: *massaging wife's shoulders*
You know
what would be sexy?
Eating food off each other...

Long awkward pause

Wife: We don't have any clean
dishes, do we?

Me: Not-a-one, no.

Date night is important for parents because they need time away from the kids, so they can talk sh*t about the kids.

My wife and I can miraculously create a human life together but this IKEA bookshelf just might kill us.

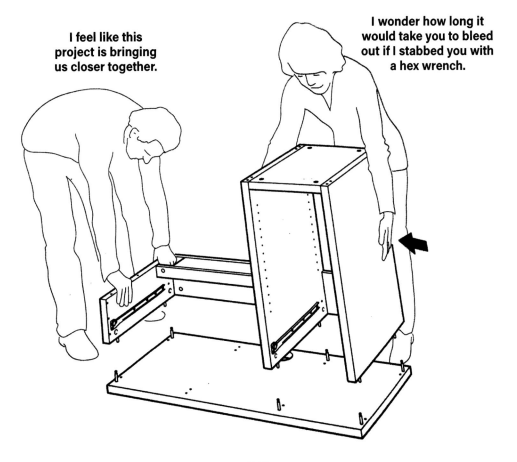

I GOT NEW GLASSES WITH ANTI-GLARE LENSES BUT I'M LOOKING AT MY WIFE RIGHT NOW AND THEY CLEARLY DO NOT WORK.

Taking turns being
the one in a bad mood

BEFORE KIDS

ARGUING ABOUT WHO GETS TO PICK THE MUSIC IN THE CAR AND WHO HAS BETTER TASTE IN MUSIC

AFTER KIDS

WOULD BE RELIEVED TO LISTEN TO LITERALLY ANYTHING YOUR SPOUSE PICKS AS LONG AS IT'S NOT THE KIDS' CHOICE

My wife wanted me to wear a vest but I'm not a vest guy so we compromised and I wore a vest.

Marriage is 50/50,
except for when
it comes to
sharing the covers.

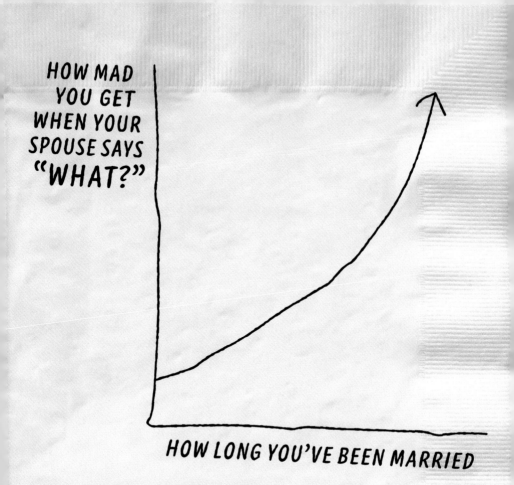

**A cooking competition show,
but all the chef's spouses are there,
somehow standing in front of whatever
drawer or cabinet they need to get into.**

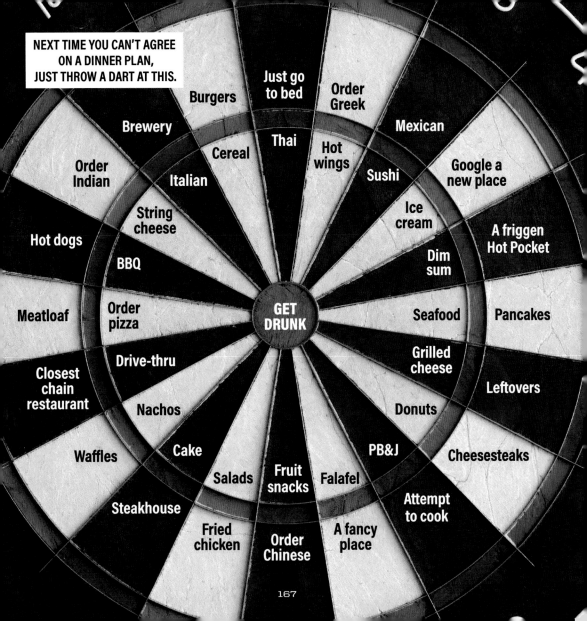

NEXT TIME YOU CAN'T AGREE ON A DINNER PLAN, JUST THROW A DART AT THIS.

167

Evil villain: I'll destroy the world unless you give me 32,000 used gift bags you've kept in a closet "just in case" muahahahaha.

Everyone: Oh no, we're doomed.

My wife: Hold my wine.

BEFORE KIDS

I'M SO TIRED OF JUST DOING DINNER AND A MOVIE FOR DATE NIGHT.

AFTER KIDS

I WOULD KILL A PERSON TO EAT A MEAL IN A RESTAURANT AND WATCH A WHOLE MOVIE UNINTERRUPTED.

Wife >

WTF IS THIS

Ha

Whoops

When your wife launches the next phase of her Closet Space Domination Plan and tries to laugh it off as an accident.

WHAT DON'T PEOPLE UNDERSTAND ABOUT THE FAHRENHEIT TEMPERATURE SCALE?

IT'S SO SIMPLE: AT 32° WATER FREEZES.

AT 212° WATER IS STILL A LITTLE TOO COLD FOR MY WIFE TO SHOWER.

As kids we wondered why our parents were always grumpy and now we're like "ohhhhh I get it."

ADULTING

Dads are young at heart. Just like our kids we love donuts, naps, and getting lollipops at the bank. Fart jokes will always be funny. We love discussing dinosaurs and monster trucks with our kids because the kid in us never really grew up (and raptors are extremely cool).

But our bodies betray us. Mysterious creaks like a haunted house, gray hair, dad bods and... oh god, is that ear hair? Instead of craving a late night on the town without kids, we're happy to doze on the couch watching a show we've seen a thousand times. We're adults in charge of paying the bills, and suddenly researching a new vacuum online takes priority over scoring tickets to a music festival.

It dawns on us that we recognize less and less of the popular songs the kids are listening to. In fact, our favorite music is starting to show up on "the oldies" station. It's over. We're not just adults, we're old. The good news is dads age like fine wine. We develop a fuller body and stronger aroma as our value increases over time (or at least that's what we tell ourselves).

BEING AN ADULT

■ Looking forward to sleep
■ Paying bills
■ Pretending I know what I'm doing

The all-consuming exhaustion I feel every day of my adult life

Caffeine

NOT MANY PEOPLE KNOW THIS BUT IF YOU CAN RECITE THE LYRICS OF AT LEAST THREE SONGS FROM THE TROLLS MOVIE THEY'LL GIVE YOU 20% OFF A VASECTOMY.

KID ME

Time to put $40 of quarters in this Pac-Man machine.

ADULT ME

LOL 99¢ for an app I will only use every day of my life? No thank you.

Growing up is basically just adding little by little to the list of sounds you make getting up from a recliner.

EVERYTHING REALLY STARTS TO CLICK WHEN YOU HIT YOUR THIRTIES. KNEES, BACK, ELBOWS... EVERYTHING.

WELCOME TO ADULTHOOD

Most of your injuries are now "sleep related."

[Racing my son]

Wife: That was really sweet how you let him win.

Me: [Did not let him win] Thanks.

KID ME

When I'm an adult I'm gonna stay up all night and eat whatever I want.

ADULT ME

If I don't finish this glass of water and get to bed by 9 I will die.

INSIDE MY BRAIN

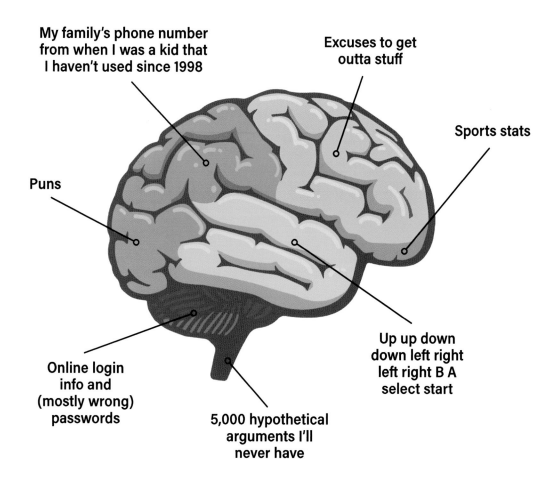

My family's phone number from when I was a kid that I haven't used since 1998

Excuses to get outta stuff

Sports stats

Puns

Online login info and (mostly wrong) passwords

5,000 hypothetical arguments I'll never have

Up up down down left right left right B A select start

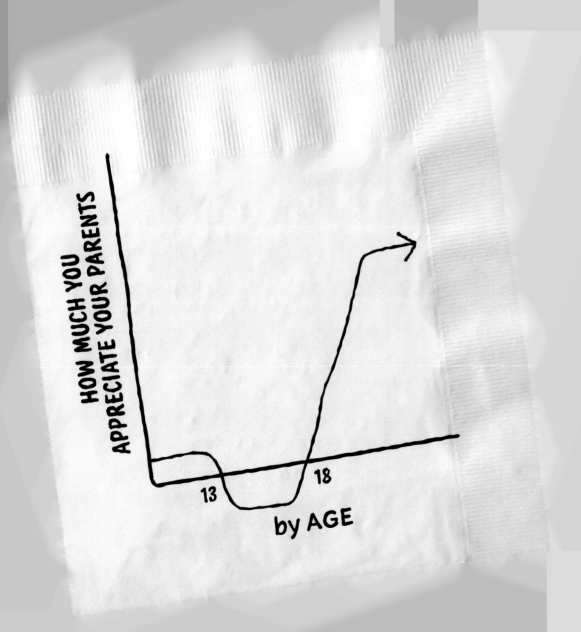

"Being a father is the least stressful job I've ever had."

—Daniel, 29

OH, YOU HAD TO WAIT 3 DAYS FOR SOMETHING YOU ORDERED ONLINE? WHEN I WAS YOUR AGE WE HAD TO WAIT FOR A PACKAGE 2 WEEKS UPHILL BOTH WAYS.

WELCOME TO ADULTHOOD
You now have a pile of comfortable clothes in the corner that you change into at night and recycle for weeks without washing.

KID ME

I'm never going to be a grumpy grown up who stresses about everything

ADULT ME

Gets furious when the grocery store changes its layout slightly

Thanks for the home improvement store gift card. I was hoping I would get chores for my birthday.

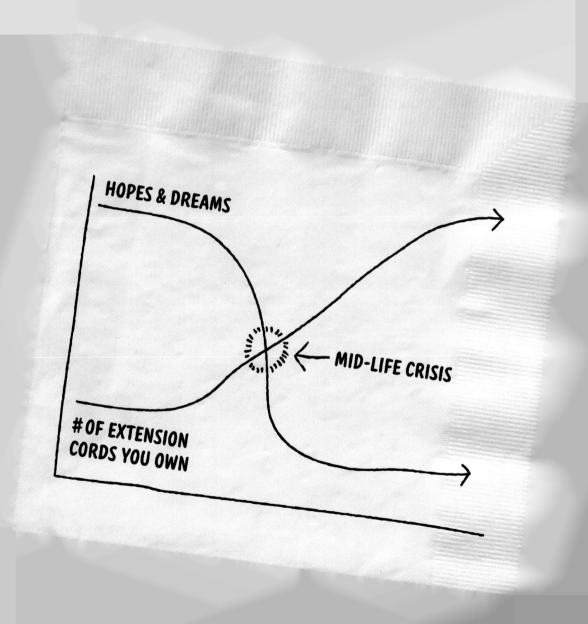

NOTHING GETS MIDDLE AGED GUYS MORE EXCITED THAN MAKING PLANS TO MEET AT A NEW BREWERY.

When you drive past your neighbor you've lived next to for 5 years but you still don't know their name.

WELCOME TO ADULTHOOD

You now have a favorite news anchor.

I've started being more honest with my son. Instead of saying "you'll understand when you're older" I tell him "when you're older you'll understand even less, but you'll also be tired."

The Kid:
Dad, I'm glad I have you. I have no idea how life works yet. I'm mostly just winging it.

The Dad:
LOL same actually.

LET'S WRAP THIS UP, WE'RE BURNIN' DAYLIGHT

Anyone can be a father, but it's riding the rollercoaster of raising a child that makes you The Dad. It's how tall you feel with your kid sitting on your shoulders to get a better view of the parade. It's holding in the "I *just* told you to be careful" when the chocolate milk spills, or tapping into your superpower ability to tune out the whining coming from the backseat. All the frustrating, funny, ridiculous, exhausting moments woven into a life you wouldn't trade for anything.

A dad is many things, but first and foremost he is THERE for his family. We are proud of our kids, our lives, our lawns, and our puns. So rock those grass-stained sneakers with pride. Because as all expert dads know, the dad club is the greatest club in the world.

Alone we can do so little; together we can do so much. (Unless there's a toddler involved, because then we aren't getting anything done.)

THE DAD

The Dad is a media brand celebrating modern fatherhood. It reaches over 100 million people per month, with membership growing every day. Welcome to the club.

AUTHORS

Joel Willis
Ally Probst
David Hughes
Jordan Stratton
Rob Whisman
Andrew Nadeau
John Darby
Tony Serafini
Brandan Moretton
Katey DiStefano
Philip Glassner
Morgan Music

James Alvarez
Sara Buckley
Mark Cognata
Jessica Czaya
Serena Dorman
Ashley Furman
Tom Gawronski
Devin Holdraker
Simon Holland
Maison Piedfort
Cian Smith
Cara Weinberger

ACKNOWLEDGMENTS

We want to thank The Dad community, everyone who follows us on Instagram, Facebook, Twitter, YouTube, and thedad.com. You make all of this absurdity possible and your support keeps us going. Thank you to our contributors for making us laugh every day.

It takes a village to raise kids, and it takes an even bigger village to run a media brand about raising kids. Thank you to everyone at Some Spider Studios for nurturing The Dad as it grew from a newborn into a mature (-ish?) adult. Special thanks to Vinit Bharara, Paul Smurl, Jimmy Applegath, Jared Warner, Mike Julianelle, Nick Fabiano, Ben Stumpf, Rob King, Matt Fisher, Ameena Usher, Geoff Isenman, Julie Steinhagen, Adam Hawkins, Sarah Rau, John Khalil, Jon Wachsman, Melissa Weingarten, Phuong Ireland, Dave Campanaro, Rachael Lubarsky, Ken Lynch, Mike Essl, and more.

Finally, thank you to our families and friends, who inspire us and let us make jokes at their expense in

Dads love inspecting a small injury like a splinter and saying, "Looks like we'll have to amputate."

Dads love saying, "That's not goin' anywhere" after tying stuff down on a truck.

But most of all, dads love being a dad.